UNEXPECTED CLEARING

Poems from this collection have already appeared in the following journals and books: *Plumwood Mountain: A Journal of EcoPoetics*, 'What Isaac Newton Saw', 'Unexpected Fall'; *Westerly*, 'Under the Wave'; *Cordite*, 'A Capella'; *Meanjin*, 'Not Here'; *Anthology of Loss* (edited by Gina Mercer and Terry Whitebeach), 'Five years and still –'; *Westerly*, 'Daughters'; and *Offset Arts Journal*, 'Adrift'.

UNEXPECTED CLEARING

Poems *by* Rose Lucas

UWA PUBLISHING

First published in 2015 by
UWA Publishing
Crawley, Western Australia 6009
www.uwap.uwa.edu.au

UWAP is an imprint of UWA Publishing
a division of The University of Western Australia

THE UNIVERSITY OF
WESTERN
AUSTRALIA

A full CIP data entry is available from
the National Library of Australia

Typeset in Bembo by Lasertype
Printed by Lightning Source
Cover photograph by Paul Bailey

This project has been assisted by the Australian Government
through the Australia Council, its arts funding and advisory body.

Australian Government

Australia
Council
for the Arts

however close our touch

or intimate our speech,

silences, spaces reach

most deep, and will not close.

Judith Wright, 'Space Between'

For my mother
Valerie Lucas
1922–2013

Contents

Night Road

Still Beating Heart

Tracking the Bay

Unexpected Clearing

A Capella:
On hearing the Tallis Scholars

Wild bird
in your cage of rib
                   and lung,
I hear you   break
                   into open space
daring
the high and unmarked air
surrounding stone,
        startling the dusty film that settles
                   across the rafters –

untrammelled soprano   reaching above
        a mesh of voice,
where human bodies
        attuned
play their notes of breath
                   pouring
                           (we were thirsty,
                           dying
                           for want of this)

streams of falling light
                   swoop   and
we ride the textured wave,
braving rapids of prayer –
                   so many hearts' ancient longings –
trusting to this crafted
                   ship of sound,
its promise of quiet water.

Balancing

To build
            or find
        a necessary poise:
            say, a white necked heron
                still
                        against the mudflats,
        watching –
this all begins
        a long way back;

Consider this tree pose,
        its deep anchor,
                        reaching branches –
        a human body,
holding,
        deceptive simplicity:

there is no last minute cram
or rearrangement
that can produce this,
that could trick the world
or ourselves
that we have roots in soil,
if we don't;

Perhaps an early tug in the weave of the ordinary –
        the practice of scales on dusty afternoons,
                virtuosity unimaginable,
an awkward conversation that finally says
        what needed to be said,
an incidental act of kindness witnessed
by no-one;
        just love's humble generosity,
                its open palm:

this quiet place
this resting,
        restless heart –

Once, in another universe, Philippe Petit set out
across the wire;
the world seemed
        solid

and yet he launched into a fitful middle space,
his body a machine for riding air and sky, for making
friends with gravity
        which let him walk,
 laughing as he danced
                light foot from element to element
knowing the precious carriage of his weight,
the even breath
the steady grip of muscle:

As dangerous and as magnificent as that –
this turning of ourselves
                with thought and craft and purpose
through time's aerial corridor,
feet curled around earthen ropes,
hands reaching for a transience of cloud.

Clearing in the Woods

One
   by one, then
severally, as breezes
      catch
at the finery of trees,
leaves
   ride the runnels of air
      down
to find the ground,
settling
in still damp grass,
a flecked universe of
   colour and shape and
      angle:

summer's dense green tunnel
done with
      already,
leaves land
like the soft footfall of
some shy creature,
looking
and treading lightly,
      then unsteadily,
through shafts of sun and now
      shadow,
these shifting woods.

Monet: Series

Giverny

Avenues of colour –
        your composed cultivations,
the fertile texture of loam
           where children have tumbled like seeds
              spilling across
your gardener's map,
its broad encompassing;

You dreamed a space –
then built in frond and petal,
        water-course and delicately
arced bridge;
and dreamed again in stroke and swathe of blue and white and
      violet and green
           floating
on the textured eye of your canvas;

so that a rippling of paint might
      transport me
now,
to that same green energy,
      translucence of light,
         the boldness of blossom,
your beloved garden.

Waterlilies

Swirl of cloud and reedy water,
smudging purple, blue,   green
of depth
        and sky –

while these lanterns
        rich vermillion
                        hover
ablaze and swinging
between shifting worlds.

Morning on the Seine

The quiet sway
                and coursing of current
as night
lapses,
where leaves trail,
        fingers through a gentler tide;
where light suffuses
                sheets of air
        slung wide across stirring water –
roiling mist,
profusion of elements:

this universe of
        bank   and   river,
a glory,
washed in strokes of white.

Lastly: Les Roses

When swirling bright pink blooms –
                clustering on leggy stems and
                        collared with rough green –
lean,
        blowsy and heavy-headed
                across a swathe of summer blue,
its cooling vapours –

vision sways and
        eddies
in the dizzying, dappled shade of the garden,
                its sighs of rise
and fall and
        quiver:

this perpetual and
                renewing
        season,
this perfumed possibility of
seeing
for the very first time.

Back Garden

All through this mild spring day
washing waves
peaceably
on the line,
      its patches of colour,
            its variables of shape
conversing equitably with little puffs of breeze,
smiling indulgently at the language of birds;

over the spires of the rosemary
      the air is thick with insects,
while a young cat cavorts,
leaping for a bee –
oblivious to harm,
in love with the daylight.

Stopped

I have let the wild machine wind down,
stopped pumping and cramming and let go
its frantic, apoplectic pulse –
its hiss and whirr and constant charge toward
some other place:

in the dusty stillness of the road,
when chequered noise has bleached into
the rustle of quiet things,
     those bedrock things that glint
         like slicked stones in the day's gentle current;
when the air curls against my face
and the feathered wings of sky are tumbling,
             white over blue –

then it is the thrum
         of a human heart that marks the place,
settling and
counting its time in beats of
touch,
and steady watching.

Reaping

Sleep's rich swathe –
where, as through the long grass of summer,
a path,
        cut and blinking in the glare,
lies down,
its generous sweep around the yard,
the inexorable travelling over the rise –

and turning like velvet amongst the stubble,
the tenacity of little flowers –
        undaunted, they lift their flushed faces
to the air,
where butterflies and small birds
        chase the movement of layers,
newly exposed:

a roiling of stars,
the deep curve of dreaming.

Bolt

The business of ordinary living
resides here also,
in this surprising geography of newness,
in this,
      for you,
                still dazzling world
of bleaching sky,
and blue grey haze of leaves
              hovering in the heat;

enlivened as you are by the unpredictability of different
people, strange places,
there is still the question
for you,
         as there is for me,
      here, as well as anywhere else,
of what is to be done with this day –

this one,
              rolled out before us like a bolt of cloth,
              vivid and
      tumbling,
the particularity of sunshine.

Orb

Today, the world is
a ripe peach,
late in the summer,
delicately furred;

its pale cheeks are
flushed
with delight:

feel
the juice flowing –
lip, to wrist,
sticky
to the elbow –

taste this world;
it is the sweetness of your
entire life.

Choir

For the Brattleboro Women's Chorus, Vermont

Ringing round and
   around the curve of the room
      our voices rise,
a surge of
   pitch and
      words
laced into
      other
         words,   layering
sound like coloured
sand
sifting in a jar;

my chest, my head ring
with fine vibrations of the air,
and our bodies
    (complex, distractable)
are, in this moment,
drawn
   in, they are
      instruments,
spokes in
a wheel of sound –

voices
turn and move,
lifting like a leaf on the breath,
the weight of the day –

listen:
this song,
a thread of sound to
circle and to
      seal these parts –
            at least
            while resonance rings and holds,
                  suspended
      in the
aching bell of the air.

Cloudless: Australian Summer

Houses crouch
        helpless,
stark
beneath the simmer
of sky;

last week's rain is all gone back
to heaven,
sucked into the aridity of nowhere,
the singed air;

fear waits
in the dusty corners of the eaves –
I hear it in the whisper of baked bark and leaf,
in the spider's spin and catch
hidden
behind the pounding of the sun.

Daughters

These girls –
they spring up at our sides,
pushing,
        lanky into the air,
    sprouting and reaching,
their leggy uncertainty suddenly
overshadowing –
while the mothers,
    faithful companions,
        solid anchor to the earth,
we only grow woodier with
intensification of event
and feeling,
the heavy swing of
many times round,
its complex gifts, its weariness;

we are walking
with these girls who were pods,
knuckled close into
a fecund dark;
we have watched the amazement of their unfurling
as seasons tumble one after another,
leaf after leaf
and hand over hand –

these girls;
their hair is as fine as corn silk
flying in turbulent currents,
the wild and surprising wind of their climbing.

Goldfields

The air hangs
still
and fragrant in
        gentle sun;

white iron-bark blossoms
stir,
they are heavy with bees;
and the heady aroma
of eucalyptus leaves and warm,
dusty earth
rises
        intoxicating
from beneath our feet.

Through the sparse trees on the
ridge up ahead,
a man comes swinging –
        pick, shovel, pan
                swag;

daylight flickers
and glimmers in the clearings,
catching
on mullock heap
and down the blackening mouths of shafts
with their shimmering, subterranean promise;

to an accompaniment of parrots,
he sings the song of the earth below –
the yellow of clay
shot through with quartz,
the reach of sinuous tree roots
groping the length
        of the dry creek bank,
or water rushing,
                clear and alluvial,
the grit that sparkles in the sunlight.

Clunes, Central Victorian Goldfields

Heat ripples
          across the wide street,
and the caps of verandahs are
pulled low
against afternoon sun;

the heaviness of
          gold   lingers
                    in the air,
stamped
in the grandness of
empty hotels,
the ornateness of a town hall façade;

but today, a dry
north wind sweeps through the town
swirling
in open doors, or
accumulating,
          in patterns of dust,
outside the closed
faces of shops, the patient houses:

the creek trickles
low
through its cracked bed,
finding its way
quietly

amongst the lunar mounds
of mullocky heaps;

but the rising fields of burnished grasses
stretch out
beneath the heady roll of the blue,
its high wisps of cirrus;

and the narrow road,
      its ragged edge lined with cypresses and
      the desolation of the wind –
         and now,
            the sudden flash of crimson rosella –
climbing
steadily to the horizon.

Friends

For Kerry Dawson

In those early times
of little sleep,
and soggy days that stretched ahead
devoid of shape and light
on comfort –
but filled with feeds, and cries,
and nappies,
and the slow,
unfolding
of learning to read the new,
small person who couldn't
read themselves –
in those blurred times
you and I became fast friends.

We pushed our prams around suburban blocks,
first with one child each
and then with two –
desperate for coffee we strained the
goodwill of neighbourhood cafes;
we chatted in each other's homes
with children, toys, food,
strewn across the mat –
and later, in parks,
talking while we pushed swings
or hovered around a little one on a slide.

I know my days were anchored
by the prospect of your company:
unadorned by drama,
we shared the flux of time –
the relentlessness of the ordinary,
the flashes of joy,
the quiet confidences in our growing children,
the hallucinatory glimpses of
another life –

How we loved to talk then
of all the things that crowd the mind –
what food is right?
what should my child be doing now?
how is it possible to soothe a wailing babe
when all I want to do is cry
and cry myself?
how these little bundles,
of tenderness and
obligation
have changed everything – all loves,
all sense of self, and
how it got so hard to just
hold on
when it wasn't clear at all
where
or what
a necessary bedrock was –

How we forge our lives even
now, transformed and
shattered
in this ongoing crucible of love and
endless division:
sharing meals, minding
children,
still talking,
still drinking coffee.

Late

A late leaf –
     falling
through shafts of thinning light –
twists in air and
     catches on frost blackened stalks;

beads of mist
     thread one by one along
          its curling points,
binding it,
     bejewelled
to earth,
     its shifting, silted layers –

seeping quietness, a
     loosening, an unravelling of borders;
this slow slip toward the steel
blue reach of cold.

Luna Park

The juddering,
the winded glee of mechanical
jolts and dips,
        deep scoop
and then the climb –

chasing the
        exhilaration to ride
as though aloft,
impervious to the quotidian of gravity –
                the earth bed, its forgotten stasis –
to be borne,
body and rush of air
indistinguishable, a moment's
single element.

High,
        beyond the palm trees, the holiday crowds
and thump of music,
the young people in their awkward beauty –
past the sandy ribbon of beach
and way out into the glitter of afternoon light –
over and
        over we ride the airy race of excitement's arc,
clutching –
its always stuttering pulse,
the swelling wave.

Conversations

A magpie pair forages in the grass beyond the stile,
black and white rumps in the air,
wings folded back in concentration
as they hunt for worms:

'maggie, maggie,'
    you coax from the verandah –
and immediately she
turns at the distinctive call
and makes a bee-line for the back door,
        a low and direct flight over the lawn;

moving decisively to each scattered piece of bacon and cheese,
her dusky
    back bobs busily –
our little velociraptor of the garden;

and when she's had her fill,
she carries a tasty piece in her beak further down the yard,
and carols,
perfunctorily,
until he swoops back down,
    strutting in his gleaming white cape
and accepts the morsel before
flying off again
    quickly
high into the branches of the narrow-leaved peppermint;

'safe' –

       he cries to his mate,

and their own wild language of wind and worms and leaves

ululates,

sweeping across the open grass,

the bending stalks.

Daylesford Massage

A stranger's fingers, knuckles, then palms
knead the oiled skin of my back,
finding the old knots –
      gnarls of muscle and bone and grip
         of scar;
            my body like a map,
    an archaeological dig through histories
        of tension, the long lineage of injury,
           the genetics of structure,
    of hours spent hunched over a desk –

wilting beneath the firm pressure of these working hands
I am transparent;
my right ovary pulses out this month's lost cargo,
its own fist of tightness,
my spine and pelvis become visible,
x-rayed to the soft music of dawn in some Japanese garden:

and my querulous, monkey mind slides to a place
    just below the surface of the water –
        its swaying reeds, the cool green underside of
    waterlily leaves –
resting,
a fish
    in dappled shallows.

Winter in Montreal

In a storeroom of the youth hostel,
in a disordered pile
of gear sloughed off or lost,
I fish out an old and ugly coat;

camouflage green, the hood
lined with fake orange fur and
grubby with
someone else's sweat and travel,
I am nevertheless grateful –
sliding my too cold body
inside its insulating skin.

Unimaginable winter:
canyons of icy air stealing
breath,
reframing the way an antipodean body
might move in the world –
      from museums to shops to cinemas and
           back to the sanctuary of the hostel –

where thought is distilled like frozen
droplets on a hood –

      watching this wandering girl
         she is
suspended in movement.

Menai Straits

To plunge into this bright stream of air –
breaking
its steamy skin;
       to launch
            into these shafts of cool blue and grey and
                mossy green –

where a single Atlantic gull,
       outlined against Snowdonia's velvet fall,
might catch the currents and
ride
       these narrow straits out
          toward an open sea.

At night, from the mainland,
the Bangor pier climbs
       plank by plank
toward our open window;
its shimmering ladders of light –
       flickers of white, green, orange –
stretch out across murmurings of inky water,
cloaking the mudflats and
       seeping like carnival music
          into the airy energy of our dreams.

South Stack, Isle of Anglesey

At South Stack,
        unfenced
                cliffs plunge
toward a steely sea,
sheer faces pocked with gulls –
        a congregation
                    nesting, watching –
while strident cries rise
        spumes of sound
                into the ozoned air;

mossed steps
        wind
in fantastical convolution
down to the lighthouse –
        an islet of green,
                the salty white of low buildings,
the bricked circumference of the tower
stark
against a battering of
sea and rock and isolation;

and all around,
an orb of hazy sky
        spreads
                wide
                        its bleaching light –
filling eyes,
        hauling heart.

The Length of Days

Our ancient cat seeks out a series of sheltered spots,
the stations of her contracting day:

on the back decking her still soft coat
shimmers in a lick of eastern light, and in the crispness of the
morning

she rolls, slow and luxuriant,
white tummy open to the air;

by afternoon, she is nested on the straw in the front garden,
crooned by the warmth of soil,

 the flick of insects
under the fronds of the lemandra;

and later, catching the last comfort from an autumn sun,
she stretches out on the dusty boards

of the verandah,
a furred crescent of contentment until

I scoop her up and carry her to her favourite evening chair
at the centre of the family room –

its yielding cushions, its possibilities of a human lap;

there, in a tight curl and tuck of tail
and paws and head,

she dreams the dreams of the long day,
its diurnal turn,

twitching in her sleep, and
receiving, as her due, our ministrations of stroke,

and murmur –
        the simple,
intricate language
                which leaps
and sparks –
from one warm creature
to another.

Eye

Viscous
jellied lens through which a
         pour of silken light
might enter me,
travelling causeways of the mind,
translating into patterns
hieroglyphs of shape –
         a filigree of bright leaves
                  quivering or
            the threaded map of your jacket as you bend
                     preoccupied, at your desk;

this humble organ,
funnelling a dazzling world:

its whisperings of colour –
         mottled greens of the hillside,
                  overlooking cobalt blue –

a still pool,
         drawing me in;
                  its dappled wavelets
troubling reflection.

What Isaac Newton Saw

At Woolsthorpe Manor,
          his childhood home,
the famous apple tree –
                    or perhaps its latter-day descendent,
          a gracious Maid of Kent –
still droops its gnarled arms toward the
clottedness of earth,
giving up its wormed and floury fruit to the grass,
to the possibilities of turbulent
and muddy transformation:

Outwitting the plague, he sat for seasons in his quiet house,
its losses and constraints,
the drabness of its close routines;
almost a poet,
he watched
with such stillness and
openness
and restlessness –
the quiet world unfolding in his garden;

an ordinary miracle that needs a different eye to see it,
          a new tilt of the head, or sudden mood of
equanimity that allows leaves to rustle,
branches to brush the lawn,
a bird to move discretely and even
          try out some autumnal singing –

each thing
        sifting into
place,
judged   or
unjudged:
until an apple simply
falls –
                a muscular movement of energy,
        and chance –
and a new constellation of elements
spins
                shimmering
into view.

Night Road

Night Road

Under moonlight's high arch
          the roll of paddocks
fall away to either side of the road,
shards of dreams only
      half woken from,
a sweeping territory of possibility,
its slivered shapes,
its lateral reach.

Still, time's route arcs forward
and complex will impels us toward morning —
      as though
           morning were another place
distinct
from the velvet of night's surrender,
from sleep's strange, adjacent space —
a somewhere country without shadow.

In Memory

After Nathan Coley

This place,
apart –
a clearing made
to mark an endless no-
where, now   no place
        to lie
but only here inside
the ache of walls, the clasp
of cold, consoling grey that runs from corner round
to corner, throwing shadows on these
greeny fields, the insects leaping in the sun –
        then slipping
                through a wedge of light, surprising opening
in summer air –
my body's width and height, its heft in space:

measured here, this slow and swaying garden makes
breath its centre piece,
the budding yarrow stalks its ticking clock,
old sundial easing into night,
while on and on the crickets' song.

Not Here

Stepping sideways out of her life
she drives to Chadstone
and checks into a suburban motel,
its beige brick anonymity a brief comfort
to muffle the racing of her pulse,
the sharp lurch of
        something else she has no name for;

in the neutral sparseness of the room,
beneath framed pictures of exotic places –
        the vivid sun of other people's lives –
she lies huddled on top of bedcovers
eyes squeezed shut
waiting,
or shutting down time, its dusty suffocations,
not moving in the unfamiliar air,
not even when her phone lights up and rings
like contact from another world:

Home:
a man and a child sit in stunned silence
in another room
        together
in another suburb,
cradling an empty handset;
another call gone through to message,
suspended in the ether like a flare –
the sparking and the hissing
of grief's long,
        descending arc.

Unkiltered

       by
the rising thought of you –

      a sudden wildness in the air;
            ozone, sultriness,
        austere chill of flurry,
the quiet, white world –

you slip my planet side-
ways,
turning its winds,
      chinook across wide plains,
human breath on frosty glass;

where a heart's fast dreaming conjures
shapes in half-light,
      darting and
stitching –
still chasing,
the elusive logic of longing.

After Bosworth Field

Richard III, the last Plantagenet King, was killed by the forces of
Henry Tudor at the Battle of Bosworth Field in 1485. His remains were
identified beneath the site of the former Greyfriars in Leicester, 2013.

Too quickly
it comes to this:
       a meagre scraping
into mud –
              not long enough –
so that your outraged man's body
       stripped to skin and gape and streaking blood
half sits, half lies,
quite broken
on this final throne:

Vaunted trophy of that frantic field –
       its wild viscera of axe and heavy sword
              the sweated force of body slammed on human body –

then
       an abject thing
   discarded here,
tied wrists
falling
       into the collapsing cradle of your lap,
black hair slimed and matted,
thick soil
       silting –
sudden emptiness
of sockets;

Shiftings
in the musty gloom:
a sedimentation of bone and mud,
metamorphosis of soil and time and
long forgetting;

the still far away ribbon
of day's
      thin and curious light.

Cool Change

The air on Albert Street
swings in our garden gate and
under the rose arbor –
      heavy now
           with clusters of quivering
pink –
straight down the musty corridor;

      the expanse of summer paddocks,
         crunch of brown grasses,
            the distant promise of
              moisture –

it swirls about the room,
calling me
    out
to ride this tempestous river
         as far as it will go,
      into the black and starry currents
of the breathing night.

Night Fog

From the bowl of the valley,
the nestling town,
mist creeps up the mountain's sleeping flank,
sinuous along the thread of road,
      its unlit curves and rocky overhangs;

          through the brambled texture of damp woods,
             panting across the crackling ice of ponds,
               visible only in the queasy
        glow of headlights
          as our small car labours
             and negotiates each turning and
      reach,
      the unexpected clearing:

Wheels crackle and slide through sludge –
and we are hopeful travellers only,
precarious
      in a glassy black.

But somewhere in these woods,
dense terrain to either side,
the tenacious possibility of home –
its modest spill of light that pools
      from porch
and window,
keeping cloud at bay,
        making a space –
hauling us in.

Over

The glory of orange that has graced our kitchen bench
for weeks now –
a vividness arching over the usual congregation of bowls and glasses
and household ephemera –
is suddenly done,
and, as though by mutual agreement,
the lillies are simultaneously coming apart –

stamens, leaves,
plump petals suddenly limp and
capsizing onto the bench and floor,
or curled in the sink,
      resigned,
at the bottom of an unwashed cup;

saffron coloured pollen
spills,
staining my hands with brightness as I gather up
the sliminess of stems
left too long in a vase,
the fluttering dissolution of such
simple magnificence –
the slowing ripple of space
in a kitchen's sudden austerity.

A Low Day

The day's bland, interminable creep:

I sit at the edge of waiting and
watching the mild
determination of the kitchen clock;

the tasks of the day are
accumulating,
a pile of untidy papers –
dusty,
like failure, they frighten me,
I have no list to hold them,
or sort them,
or beat them into a thing I could say was mine;

potential
        slips through my fingers
like spilt milk,
a stale scum of reminder coating
idle hands.

Stones

Sliding into sleep, I am back
on the road I walked today, through
arcades of heady gold and

russet, swirls of leaves alive
in air and crisp underfoot, even
through the persistence of light rain.

This road hugs the curve of a hill –
woodlands to one side and a
field below; both are criss-crossed with the

broken lines of old stone walls,
weathered and grey and speckled with lichen.
The stones balance, nestling under and

over one another, cupped
together like fractious parishioners,
the severe tablets of their faces

scoured into blankness
by the relentless wheel of seasons.
Talismans,

residue of farm and clapboard house
long since contracted into
cellar holes, those sunken

places all overtaken now
by the dappled green of moss,
by the endless drifts of matted leaves.

Who laboured here? Their footsteps
mark out the boundaries of this field,
harvesting its rich,

and sometimes meager, promise:
tilling soil, tending to animals,
a child balanced on a hip,

building, always building,
stone upon stone,
the mottled layers of their lives.

Adrift

All through night's long and
unsupported hours –

ocean's pitching black, its surge and scoop,
the power of its flick and suck
relentless flick and suck –

Barely seaworthy, a boat
lurches
         too low in inky slops,

staggering:
a heavy press of bodies in
queasy shades, an intimacy of faces where

stories grip –
the small hands of children –

around necks, fingers –
                voices

desperate across
         blank water –

words swallowed
in a heaving dark.

Sirens

For Martin Harrison

Bees mass
    frantic
        in the column of the tree, they

are thick in the webbed mesh of green and I
    am bound by the furious sound of
        secret lives, wild and

focused;
    harmonic they vibrate
        low into the balmy channels of the air,

ratchetting at my sternum,
    a contrapuntal shaking,
        an epileptic ecstasy,

a thousand tongues of hieroglyphic sweetness –
    the hypnotic,
        honeyed pulse of danger.

Tropic

When tropic darkness
                    drops
a sudden sheath over the closeness of day,
          heat's persistent thrum

when the raucous calls of night birds
rustle the fronds,
unsettling the quiet
in the same way that currents stir the sand,
drawing up flecks and eddies into the clear water –

I turn to find you –
the warm, travelled terrain of your body
still swimming
under the lightest sheet.

Under the Wave

Slipping under the wave –
that space where even sand
might settle,
     unswirled, where
the turbulence that rakes at the roots of your hair
     filling it with grit,
         yanking it back toward the wildness of the surface,
a kind of reverse gravity,
might yet,   like the hand of god,   pass over you –

slip under the wave,
you know its towering confluence of tide and wind,
the crushing hammer of its foamy fist;
watch, where the form of your flailing, human body,
with all its intricacies of angle and organ,
might turn its fins in this mottled light,
negotiating an ancient element –

slip under the wave,
make for the sky.

Winter, on the Hamilton Highway

Travelling early, cloud settles across
sodden paddocks,
        dampening the sun;

a close grey world where
only the nearest landscapes
emerge
        momentarily
into focus:

sweeping past fields   rocky
        or cleared, where stones have been hauled
to perimeters,
sometimes shaped into rough walls;

a scatter of sheep
or, later, the lumbering shapes of cows
clustering on the grass,
churning runnels of mud around the gate;

a country house braced against the seep of cold,
the encroachment of the fields;
smoke threads from
a morning fire,
breath into the icy air:

pale yellow sun slowly
breaking in,
unpeeling the day,
its muted glory.

Hidden Pole

This dreaming place,
  cold underside,
creaking in opacity,
plank and floe –

how will I know you
again
in the meek light of temperate day?

Your cloaked peaks,
  groaning citadels of ice,
they loom like stars or
    sudden ships in blackness,
bearing down –

remembering the tug
of ocean pits where
thoughts
    flicker and
  glide –
metallic ghosts
to ride invisible tides,
imagining an easy surface.

Vacant Places

'I felt regretful to have been compelled to turn back, as the lure of the
ridges was strong, and the vacant places seemed to beckon irresistibly.'

Frank Hurley, Photographer; Antarctic diary, December 21, 1912.

Illegible landscape,
white page
empty of inscription
we crawl across your indifferent face –
interlopers,
pirates;

impervious to metaphor your
vacant places
call
and repel me,
siren songs of jolting ridges,
flattening blasts of frozen wind,
blue abyss of the crevasse
that speechless,
creaking vault:

what does my human eye
have to do with this vast place,
this counterpoint
      below the northern bear
these flickering southern lights
illuminating strangeness?

our anchoring pole,
empty of mirrors
untrackable continent –
      you resist our compositions.

And yet, the wonder of this turning

During my last year of high school
I was suddenly alert to the
coming of spring –
as though,
through all the charmed years of childhood,
spring had never quite
happened before;

but this year,
I saw in sharp relief
the cupped hands of the magnolia –
resplendent in suburban gardens,
its snow drift brushed
with bright magenta –
fragile,
      bold;

and the curl of the jasmine vine
as it draped,
rampant
over the fence,
      the impossible
beauty of its perfume
wreathing around my heart's tight clench –

autumn's lost and shimmering sac of tissue and blood still
indelible;
its new grim thread
to course through every pattern

in the wash of my life,
a bass note to sound
heavy
even here,
in the brightness of the year's turning:

and yet, the wonder of this turning;
the curious lift of the body
toward the strange
		possibilities
of gusty air,
the sweet tenacity of leaf bud,
the soul's
		unexpected
 season of rich
unfurling.

Natura Morta

In this framed   space
the breathing world is
clasped
a moment,

                its frantic pulse soothed and
carefully composed –

    swirl of petal,
        its smudging pinks
          drooping
against the dark belly of a vase,
 supper laid out on a pewter plate,
        the heavy loaf, a cross-hatched piece of cheese –

     translucence
   in a spray of light,
the lacquered depths,
a quivering stillness.

Burning

February 7, 2009

Ravenous:

for the dryness of grass,
the crackle of trees and
twists of
      melted metal
abandoned
where whole forests
      blazing
have crashed across a mountain road;

for the flickering
      embers of somebody's
home,
a desolation of scorch and smoke –

and for the softness of the child who is cradled,
desperately –
      fragility of skin, wisps of singed hair –
she is held against the roar,
the rage of racing heat –

and now the mother –
her child,
her child's children:
pacing at the emergency shelter,
she pins increasingly urgent notes to a makeshift board:
'Where are you? Call me' –

Sick with fear
mouth dry
this maddening
this acrid drift of ash –

Every Thing

Every
thing in this fine and
complicated world
    asks
to be considered;
every creature
        breathing,
or moving,
or just passing,
patiently,
through the flickery, deep-sea caverns of time,
    waits to be held
in the eye
of someone's
attention:

say, the green needles of the pine that
    arc,
tentatively,
toward heaven;
the air,
heavy with impending storm
that sweeps over the grasses,
        stirring
them to some wild and
tremulous action;

or a child's warm, rough
palm pressed

briefly
against your own:

this sweet unfolding
of looking
   and loving
        and letting be.

In the Louvre

To know the shining world
of skin and breath,
abstraction of thought and desire
                transubstantiated
into the gesture of a hand,
the luminosity of marble flesh –

or the way in which a smear of pigment
       and painstaking brushstrokes
might render the motility of a human face,
its longings,
a chiaroscuro of the mind –

an interior life
made visible –
then given wings.

These Hands

These hands,
not as beautiful as perhaps
        they once were –
have nevertheless learned a finer art
than elegance:

see how they curl around the arc of your shoulder
in the quietly breathing night –
fingers stroking warm smoothness in
a language of intricate connection,
whatever the hour;

or the arch of wrist,
the straining of tendons
        raising fingers
onto keys,
loosing sequences of sound in
that delicate marriage of body and
instrument –
        the wild clasp of giving
and taking;

or now,
        where fingers, thumb and palm cup
                to hold and draw this pen –

see, it quivers like an arrow,
poised
ready to fly and find out
                the fleeting mark.

Unexpected Fall

Barn doors are latched against the snow
and a slash of red roof slants across winter's pale, oncoming
      frame:
when a grouse,
      flecked and surprisingly elegant
            sails low through the yard,   hitting
doors with crunch of bone,
the rupturing sac –
so that an angularity of feathers slides
slow toward the still exposed gravel of the drive,
trailing bloodied tracks to answer
gravity's obscured urgings,
the density of this clotted earth;

even as the honeyed light of lamps
 springs up in human windows –
         the silken weave of feather and warm body,
           the airiness of skeleton, acuity of eye,
              flight's bold trajectory –
all fall askew,
broken and
cooling already as evening
floods the wide and darkening fields of death's wilderness –
its blackening grasses,
its blank interruption.

Still Beating Heart

Still Beating Heart

My Mother in Hospital

Before she catches sight of me in the doorway of the busy ward
I see my mother;
she is perched on the edge of her hospital bed,
glancing distractedly out the window and over the tin and
                                        terracotta roofs of the city,
now tapping her slippered foot,
her knotted fingers pulling at a bedraggled tissue.

I see that she is polite but impatient with the solicitous
sweeping past of the nurses –
their meds and blood pressure machines and
cups of stewed, tepid tea –
but mostly I see she is cross with the walking aid
that waits,
ignored but inevitable,
in her corner of the room,
its gifts of mobility
obscured
by a vision of age,
of some old woman pushing a frame.

Bar by bar,
infirmity builds its cage around her –
the creep of heart attack, a fall, arthritis,
the fading of memory's foreground, the
poisonous slips of mind and mood;

she beats her frail body against it,
railing, pretending:
and who can blame her?

Although most of our history together is
conflicted,
she is still the one who cared for me
as I care now for my children,
their soft skin and bright eyes the delight
of all my days,
my body and my love the unspoken anchors of their lives –
as she was mine.

I am bringing her a bag of mandarins –
the bright orange of their skins glows,
pungent,
in the antiseptic neutrality of the ward;
looking up, she smiles,
catching their freshness on the air.

Afternoon Rest

Snagged
      on the day's reedy currents,
         the trudge of chores,
she gathers up her small child to lie
beside her on the wide bed;

she gentles with stroking hands and deepening breath,
hoping
to weave sleep's hypnotic spell
over restless limbs,
determined brain;

while weariness draws her
      heavy and fast,
         her body's weight an impress on the chenille quilt
as the moorings of wakefulness are loosed –
surfacing just enough to catch the twist,
the would-be flight of
      unsubdued energy.

Now,
I feel how tired you must have been,
know for myself the irresistible miracle of sleep;
now, I stroke you,
      my dear,
your knotted hands,

these wisps of hair,
the worry still creasing your forehead,
misting the violet of your eyes;

at last,
we speak together
this late and
long-remembered language
        of breathing
                and closeness
and different journeys.

Falling

There is no calm here   only
this night-gowned flail of
terror that
      collapses
a hollowness of empty space –
           not
           a slipping into the kindness
               of closing water
but

clinging to the bathroom rail
she won't be moved,
cries out
      convulsed
for each of her children
numbered – these fragments, only –
then, howling
again for Kenny
           where is he?
               (gone   intolerable)
or Sam
oh, where's my father, Sam?
can't bear –

Still beating heart.

Her eyes are squeezed
shut
shut to the witness of white tiles
     the walking frame
to the nurses,
hovering
     trying their best –

With startling ferocity
she grips my hand:
     it stands in for everyone,
     everything.
     It's not enough.

No calm here   only
the desperate sting of syringe
     slurring sobs,
only another kind of
drowning,
     piecemeal –

The Call

In dawn's blue hour, the roads to the hospital
        slide into motion
like swimmers into a pool
                    the whoosh of water
                      the slow build
as the great pulse of the city
        jolts,
            the day's
rising adrenalin;

hot air balloons
            hang,
inverted teardrops
                over the bridge,
      the wide plain of concrete and glass,
           the slick of river, its dusty banks –
and small flames erupt,
        flaring;
high above me, someone is watching,
someone wrapped in the freshness of gusting air –
a different kind of morning:

I find you
barely lipping the surface;
        you curl,
curtained away and
              cocooned

in cords and tubes,
the quiet riff of beeping machines;

     already adrift on a slow wash,
my sister and I cradle your hands,
 we whisper to you love's full
          and unremarkable story,
its wondrous repetitions,
     hoping you can hear us;

the elusive graciousness of
         this letting go –
this hard unravelling.

Full Fathom

In the slow
        quiet hours that
follow midnight,
        when darkness dips down into
                its deepest trough –
                        the long tide turns,
                                catching
                the precious husk and
                        bearing you
                silent and changing,
                        on foam and wash, the bier
                                of night –

away from the narrow beach of our lives,
        its cooling sand, its clamour
                and its longings;

a remnant flickering of figures –
        neptune's necklace, a spiraling shell –
                all slipping gentle,
this final,
        watery element.

Death of an Artist

In a paint-stained black folio,
we find your last paintings –
your working thoughts,
not brought to completion:

colour still in undiffused blocks behind
a sketchy figure
fishing from some rocks,
the river already brown and vast;
or the country house,
its slanted tin roof
        catching morning sun
against a damp green of bush,
chickens pecking in the foreground,
not quite to scale:

or in your sketchbook,
careful exercises in pencil –
the quiet beauty of a model's body posed,
        then turning –
I see that you saw the miracle of flesh and spirit;
you were carefully unveiling,
paying it homage.

Then, in the hospital, the day you cried –
raw, terrible –

because somehow you recognised
you wouldn't paint again;
I held your hand,
I knew you knew.

And later in the nursing home we brought you paint and pencils but
all you would draw was a strange abstraction of two figures,
blurred together;
I wondered what bifurcation you imagined or,
in my more sentimental moments,
whether you were rejoining my father,
your long life's coupling.

I remember you leaning across your table,
       amid an inevitable scatter of brushes and unlidded
          tubes of paint and smeared
             glasses of water,
angling the lamp over your work and
coaxing clawed fingers toward
wash
      and shade, the commitment
         of line –

you were loving the idea –
      the world refracted through the particularity of the image –

you were drawing it into the light.

Faltering

For Betty Malpas

Through each slow day of your dying –
    as our shared planet slides in a confusion
      of shadow and gleam,
        faltering as time –
we took calls,
made dull sense of an accretion of details,
came to know the failing of far-away winter light:

helpless to do anything else,
we sifted through photos:
    your many trips to us,
intrepid and sunburnt –
    or, here, cosy before your own fire,
    slippers, cardigan drawn close,
      the pleasure of tea in china cup and saucer,
        the quiet order of your English bungalow.

How atoms love to congregate –
    these transient galaxies of moments, bend of faces,
grief's abiding cast, each shimmering,
      enlivening point of joy –

a swathe of fine lace laid out across the reaches of this warm,
protracted space –

      unstitching now and
      dissolving into darkening air –

leaping molecules of flame,
the patient grace of life's insistent making
and unmaking.

What Remains

When, in dreams, he sees her,
there is no longer any need to try
to recall –
      say, the way she raised one eyebrow in arch surprise,
      or the sharp angles of her body
                turning in mirth, or precision –
nor be limited to those closely studied moments of her face
that are framed on the walls of their house,
or perhaps lurk inside boxes, or someone's camera,
those fixed images of a life
        so full of movement and sparkle it is still
the pulsing current of his own –

when, some nights,
      she comes to him in dreams –
a sometimes grace he can't call up –
he can relax at last
      and simply watch her,
joy and relief flooding him in equal measure;
her mouth shapes words,
        the loved face bending
      close through the slipperiness of what can't quite
          be seen –

but even though he strains,
pressing at the edges of his dream
to hear,
her meaning always stays
      just out of reach,

a voice dulled beneath a heaviness
of tumbling water –

Still, it's enough to make the waking
        almost bearable,
the relentless re-entry into desolation
        new, always impossible –
just his own tired breathing in the familiar bedroom,
in the grey, straggling light of early morning,
always too early.

Five Years and Still –

Five years –
and still there are days when
I want to pick up the phone and
call you;
time seeps by,
and though grief
      loosens its cruelest hooks
I remain bereft,
      perplexed –
where are you?

Are you still sitting at your computer
tapping out the stories of your life –
      the boy in the Queensland bush,
         the young man stationed
in Darwin,
poring over radar?

Or will I see you
coming into the kitchen –
      a cup of tea in the offing –
joining us around the table,
the arc of your arms
still
wiry and strong?

And if I could get a line
      through to you –
what would I say?

The children are growing,
             beautiful,
I left my job,
the old cracks in the family
widen and groan like
lathe and plaster in the drought –
I admit we are all
             diminished
without you.

Most of all,
unreconciled,
I would ask you to
come home –
it's enough now,
             please
come back –

And here it is again:
the persistence of that old,
mad dream of
restoration,
when the patience of mourning,
the gratitude
for all the rich
             love you left amongst us –
gives way
to the shocking
             need for the miracle:

the past

          intact and

    cupped

in the broad palms of your sun-tanned hands.

Miss Hilda's Walk

Hilda Leviny (1883–1981) was the last surviving member
of the two generations of the Leviny family who lived at
'Buda' in Castlemaine.

I am the last of my
             overflowing generation –
our long carved table crowded
with a generosity of parents, brothers,
       all of my sisters -
our voices drifting in corridors,
or settling like wood smoke
                  around comfortable chairs while
every room fills with the quiet
hum of private plans,
our industries of contentment.

It is my lonely honour
to wait here,
in a corner of this now
too quiet house,
       its draughty spaces,
where pale sun can still warm me through stippled glass,
where I can watch the garden ramble,
       spilling
             into autumn –

I have been trying to will my aching hands
to pen, even back to needle –
but they falter,
don't know their way,
there is hardly any thread left to pull –

and still
the others press against me
        close
like cats
or perhaps little eddies of wind,
stirring the curtain –
each now come to their own
particular finishing,
 each distinct strain
fallen
into the opacity of silence,
unstitching the brocade of our lives,
thinning the season's cooling air.

In these late days,
when mist and
penumbra
start to creep across our hill –
        its briars,
                the proud cypress hedge –
I dream of a time when branches will reach over
the secret pathways of my walk
and I will meander there again,
no longer visible from the house,
gone into the hidden garden –

        their faces –
                turning and
quickening

through the fading brambles of the japonica,
brushing my cheek,
calling my name –
      to the glory of wild roses,
            to springtime's forgotten tapestries.

Tracking the Bay

Beach Road

I never gave my heart to you,
or meant to;
but the curve of the bay
caught me –

     the view away
   from the road and the traffic lights
   and down to the beaches
     sometimes the sweep of sand,
        or clusters of grey rocks protruding
          into lapping water –
even the squawking of silver gulls
soothed me,
spoke to me of something else:

Parallel to the business of my day –
this glimpsed promise of the misted horizon,
the siren song of the light,
and the rain
    falling and
rising
like curtains
on another stage.

End of the Season, Port Melbourne

A sudden, chill wind,
heavy with salty spray,
whips up Bay Street –
chasing bare shoulders and
sunglasses around corners and
down alley ways like
damp,
scurrying leaves.

Behind the shivering fronds of the palm
tree at the end of the road,
sky and sea are almost
indistinguishable –
surging blue-gray bands
      they hover,
              glistening
above the beach,
as vertical shafts of rain
advance
      bold
across the haze of the horizon.

Kulin Country

After James Boyce, 1835

Stand at the crossroads and look,
Ask for the ancient paths,
Ask where the good way is, and walk in it
Jeremiah 6:16

Once a reach of grasslands,
            undulating and
        mapped to the scope of human eyes or
                an arm's expansive encirclement –

an efflorescence of herbs, a delicacy of orchids
        pushing through tussocks,
nodding shyly in dappled light;

birds flying low over wetlands
        stalking in mud,   rustling amid clumps of reed;
their cries ring out across

                this gathering place
of talk
and feast,
rich confluence of waters,
        salty and fresh:

New city –
        a magnificence of towers,
                vibrant babel of voices –

hauled from the trample of ancient paths,
theft's violent swathe;

listen to
           the haunting sweetness of wind
                                still coursing
                through spring grasses,
the forgotten voices rippling
           across this same
                     wide circlet of sea.

Midnight, Inner West

The sounds of the docks
travel across gritty expirations of the night city,
over galvanised roofs and spectral
backyards, over late night office workers –
      here, the click of a lamp, spilling
           its circle of light, there the blue glow
                of a computer –
and over the crazy swerve of
headlights
      channelling down empty streets:

The sounds of the docks slide in through the open window,
harnessing shifts in air –
      meanwhile we stir and touch,
      turning on warm sheets –
while the great haul and clank of hull
reverberates
on wharf,
the metal hulks of shipping containers
grinding,
tossed in the massive claws of the gantry.

In my salty, oil-slicked dreams, the river
glints black,
      an open passage
the wild and trackless swell beyond the Bay.

Container Ship

Stacked high with coloured boxes
the huge ship manoeuvres
        through the narrow channel of the Heads
and into the Bay,
a small pilot boat
nudging it toward the city
and the port;

its bows,
        which must have risen to meet the wild, high surge
                of trackless sea,
now gently break these meek,
domestic waters,
and the masts of the little boats at Williamstown
tinkle and wave,
bobbing
as this grand hulk of rust and steel
slips below
        the massive sweep of the bridge
and on toward the waiting gantries –

their vast metallic arms
ready
to receive and
        segment
these strange and precarious
fruits of the open ocean.

Summer Evening, Point Gellibrand

At low tide, the grey rocks –
       threaded with groove and cracks and
              streaked with seaweed's soft, slippery greens –
sigh, and heave their slicked shoulders
clear of the thrum of the sea;

cratered pools emerge into the steam
of salty air,
their small worlds
       suspended in
scoops of flickering light and sand:

       the jointed sway of neptune's necklace,
       the anxious burrowing of crabs back into sand,
              scuttling out of sight;
       the sculptured accommodations of shells, some piecemeal,
       some whole,
       the tip of a shard of coloured glass,
       smoothed and opaque,
       turned over in my giant's hand.

Picking our way in sandalled feet
we follow the sensate push and suck of the sea –
       this edge, this narrow strip;
searching,
our faces take quivering shape in little mirrors,
licked by the wind.

Altona Beach

Beyond the belching flames of the refinery,
       its skeletal frame,
a long slap of wave
           sounds
 up and down the wide sandy reach,
stitching
a petticoat of foam
       onto the hem of the beach –

spray rises up
into the bright cathedral of the day,
and a light tattoo of ozone
and ocean
tracks
across hot skin;

out of the sun's glare,
the children swim into shadows under
the old pier –
its legs crusted
with barnacles,
joints clamped together with rusted
hinges –
waving
     they head
         further out,
splashing through softly lapping,
translucent water;

launching their bright bodies
        off the pontoon,
the cascade of their voices
        wafts back to
where I sit,
watching,
my toes in the sand,
        my thoughts
floating like clouds
in a dome of fierce blue.

At the Borrow Pit

on the Western Treatment Plant, Werribee – a wetland area of
international significance
For Shirley Cameron

A surprising swerve away
        from the stretch of the Geelong Road, its rush
from city to city –

                        to find the paddocks
                    sloping down toward an unimagined
        remoteness
of coastline
                its shelled beaches,
                the stink of seaweed –

In a purposeful wilderness of pond
                        and grassy bank,
of drain and gate,
water birds gather
        and leave,
fan out across the dreamy expanses of
elsewhere and
return,
                dipping their beaks;

A meditation of watching
        from the bench at the bend in the track,
where cherry wort creeps across a patchiness of green
and wavelets chase,
        peaking
                across the lagoon –

And we see three pelicans circle
                    and settle
in gargantuan glide,
while a congregation of red-necked stints
turn their tiny,
          proud backs to us,
                    facing into an afternoon wind.

Stranded

William Buckley 1837, two years after his reabsorption into
European society after 32 years with the Wathaurung community
on the Bellarine Peninsula.

I have stood a long time
       waiting
by this river bank,
its muscular brown body
twisting and writhing like a snake;
I have watched daylight rise and fade
many times,
and night spring like a raven
over the plains,
flying down onto
beaches
and into the mouths of rocky caves;

Only two things I know:
the smoky smell of what is familiar
             and the precious,
fading life on the other bank –
                inked skin
                riven heart –

Adrift
by this brown river,
       not in this place
       or that,
there is only the promise
           of raven's low swoop
the hypnotic pulse of his blue-black span,
its midnight seep of forgetfulness.

Between the Heads

Alongside the white flank of the ferry –
    its open deck of parked cars,
    its milling of travellers,
        faces behind glass or laced
            with wind and salty spray –
two dolphins dive and leap
        through the swell,
playing in the foamy wake.

For all our going forward –
            as the jut
    of one pier reaches round to grasp
  the next,
    holding fast,
    drawing in –
this is the space between
        suspended and riding above
the tension of channel and tide;

a momentary pleasure of flight
in glinting sun,
skimming a stippled horizon of water.